50 Ways To Promote Your Book

NICKY MARSHALL

&

SHARON CRITCHLOW

Manuscript produced in the United Kingdom. No part of this book may be used or reproduced in any manner without written permission except in the case of brief quotations embodied in critical articles or reviews.

Although we have made every reasonable attempt to achieve complete accuracy in the content of this book, we assume no responsibility for errors or omissions.

These tips are intended to inspire, rather than advise. This book is not intended to be, or replace, expert advice. It is simply a collection of practical promotional techniques discovered through years of book launches and author support. You should always consult a professional about your own circumstances.

Copyright © 2023 DISCOVER YOUR BOUNCE PUBLISHING

All rights reserved.

ISBN 978-1-914428-16-6

DEDICATION

This book is dedicated to everyone who has put pen to paper and shared their creation. Every book has a bit of the author imprinted in it and placing your thoughts, experience or creativity in the public realm is an act of vulnerability. This book is dedicated to your bravery and to your ongoing success in sharing your book with the world.

CONTENTS

Foreword	1
Introduction	5
GET READY!	**10**
Tips 1–10	11
Promotion Strategy One: Rebecca Jenkins	23
GET EXCITED!	**28**
Tips 11–20	29
Promotion Strategy Two: Jenny Lewis	41
KEEP GOING!	**45**
Tips 21–30	46
Promotion Strategy Three: Helen Blenkinsopp	59
TIME FOR A REFRESH?	**63**
Tips 31–40	64
Promotion Strategy Four: Rich Collis	77
MORE AMAZING IDEAS	**80**
Tips 41–50	81
Bonus Strategy Five: Joel Stone	93
About Discover Your Bounce!	98
About the Authors	101

FOREWORD

Fellow writers, authors and book lovers,

Joel Stone here, and I'm thrilled to be introducing you to 50 Ways to Promote Your Book. Now, before you roll your eyes and groan about yet another book on marketing and promotion, let me tell you this – if you're expecting your book to take off like a rocket without any effort from your side, you're in for a disappointment.

As a marketing entrepreneur, international speaker and bestselling co-author of Stay Hungry, I know first-hand that a book on its own won't change your world. You've got to promote it, promote you, make sure it's seen, get it out there in the world, share it and shout it from the rooftops. Okay, maybe don't shout from the rooftops, but you get my point.

It's no secret that writing a book is hard work. It takes time, dedication and a whole lot of caffeine to get to the finish line. But once you've written 'The End', the real work begins. You need to promote your book and let people know it exists. Because let's face it – your book won't sell itself.

That's where 50 Ways to Promote Your Book comes in. This book is packed with practical tips, tricks and strategies to help you get your book in front of your target audience. And the best part? You don't need a marketing degree or a massive budget to implement them.

Whether you're a self-published author or have a traditional publishing deal, this book will help you boost your book sales, increase your visibility and grow your author platform. You'll learn how to leverage social media, email marketing, book bloggers, podcasts and much more.

But here's the thing – promoting your book isn't just

about sales. It's about connecting with readers, building relationships and creating a community around your book. It's about showing the world what you're passionate about and why your book matters.

So, don't let the fear of self-promotion hold you back. Embrace it. Because when you're promoting your book, you're promoting yourself. And you deserve to be seen, heard and celebrated.

Now, I know some of you might be thinking, "But Joel, I'm an introvert. I don't like self-promotion." Trust me, I get it. As a (loud) introvert myself, the idea of putting myself out there used to terrify me. However, you don't have to be an extrovert to promote your book.

Promoting your book is about finding your unique voice, your message and your story. It's about connecting with your audience authentically and genuinely. And let me tell you – there's nothing more powerful than an author who's passionate about their book.

So, my fellow writers, authors and book lovers, I

encourage you to read 50 Ways to Promote Your Book with an open mind and a willingness to take action. Don't just read it – implement it. Try out the strategies that resonate with you and see what works.

Remember, promoting your book isn't a one-size-fits-all approach. It's about finding what works for you and your book. And with 50 Ways to Promote Your Book as your guide, I'm confident you'll find the right path to success.

So, go ahead and dive into this book. Let it be your companion on your author journey. And most importantly, let it remind you that your book deserves to be seen, heard and celebrated.

Stay hungry!

Joel Stone

INTRODUCTION

Congratulations, you have written your book!

Maybe you have self-published…

Maybe you have a publisher…

But after the initial joy of seeing your words in print many authors feel disappointed with their book sales. It's not surprising that it can be hard for your book to be found given that Amazon releases **over 1.4 million** self-published books through its Kindle Direct Publishing platform every year. There are **33 million titles listed on Amazon** as of February 2022, and this is only one route to market. The book market is a busy place, but there are people out there who are seeking what you wish to share.

The great news is that the Booksellers Association reported in 2022 that their membership of independent book retailers had increased for the fifth consecutive year. So, there are many ways your book can find its forever home.

This book is 50 ways to find your audience and engage with them. It is written by two Amazon best-selling authors who have helped many others to engage with their readers and become bestsellers themselves. These are tried and tested methods for you to apply to your book. We have also included some real life case studies written by other authors on how they have sold or utilised their books.

How to use this book

We have categorised these 50 ideas for ease of access.

1. **Get Started!** This covers the period of time before you launch.
2. **Get Excited!** This is about the launch process.
3. **Keep Going!** This is marketing your book.
4. **Refresh Your Book!** If your book sales are slowing down, take a look at this section. It could also be called Marketing Part Two.
5. **More Amazing Ideas!** We had so many ideas we put the rest of them in this section.

The book has been written to take you and your book on a journey and much will depend upon your success to date as to where your journey begins. We would recommend that self-published authors start at the first section as this addresses how the world sees your book and its appeal.

Don't restrict yourself to going in order – take a random tip and run with it for a few weeks!

Approach each group of tips with a sense of fun.
Involve your friends, family and followers as much as you
can. Persistence is the key, some of these tips need to be
repeated over a period of weeks or months. Some tips are
one off actions.

Further help

We are Discover Your Bounce Publishing.

You can find us at:

www.discoveryourbouncepublishing.com.

We create, launch and relaunch books all of the time

and would love to cheerlead your book!

Engage with us on social media.

www.facebook.com/groups/bouncybooks

www.linkedin.com/company/discover-your-bounce-

publishing

50 Ways To Promote Your Book

Use the hashtags #50booktips for our support!

Sources

www.tagari.com/how-many-books-are-published-on-

amazon/

www.booksellers.org.uk/industryinfo/industryinfo/latestn

ews/Number-of-independent-bookshops-in-BA-

membership-i

GET READY!

Tip #1: Get clear on your vision

What do you want your book to do for you?

At every stage of your book journey, take a few moments each day to visualise your book journey:

- People smiling as they buy and read your book.

- You smiling as you receive your royalties.

- Lovely reviews.

- Being on stage or presenting your content.

- Getting into newspapers or magazines.

- Other exciting opportunities.

- More books!

The opportunities are endless, really get into the positive emotions of your book journey. It can help initially to connect with a memory of something lovely that happened, then switch your attention straight to your book, carrying those positive feelings with you. There are lots of resources and books on visualisation and the Law of Attraction if you want to read further.

Tip #2: Create your brand image

Take some time to review your website and socials to ensure your branding is consistent. The look and feel of every interaction you have with your audience should be the same. Choose a palette of colours and images, or work with a designer to help you.

Make sure your book and social links all work on your website and newsletter – broken links are missed opportunities!

Tip #3: Amazon profile

With so many books being published, your reader will want to see activity that means your book is in demand. Your book page should be vibrant, with good descriptions and reviews – preferably with a picture.

Your Amazon Author Central Profile is another place to connect with your reader. Take your time to complete this and ensure you shout about the benefits of reading your book.

Tip #4: Where does your book live?

Do you have a website for your book?

Even a one-page website can make a difference, as it allows you to be found by search engines. It also gives you the opportunity to get sign ups to your email or your business service.

A one-page website should have branding which matches the style of your book and have the following:

- A picture of your book

- A link to buy your book on Amazon or other platforms

- A description of what the book is about

- Reviews of your book

- Contact details for you or your publisher

- A sign up option for details of your next book and/or your services

- Your social media links

You could also add a video of you describing your book or providing an outline of the story as a teaser.

Tip #5: Check your sales channels

Look at the information you have about the sales you have already had. What is the method of purchase? Is it direct through Amazon, via a book store or your own events? Are people choosing ebooks or paperback?

Take some time to understand your customer and how they want to buy from you. Also think of how you can reach new markets with what is working for your current audience. It can be an idea to create an avatar of your ideal client, so you can think about where they are, offline and online.

Tip #6: Geographical promotional strategy

Different countries tend to use different types of social media. Our research has showed that LinkedIn isn't as popular as Twitter in some places in the world, so do your research by region and age group, and pick the right channel for your target customer.

It may be that you choose two or three different channels per country to post your content. Try to be consistent and remember your call to action!

Tip #7: Nielsen

Is your book listed on Nielsen? This is a way of getting it seen by a wider distribution base. WH Smith, Waterstones and other large retailers look at this listing for their books.

Nielson has a free listing option, which allows you to provide a short description and to tag it according to the type of book. You can also upload a cover.

A distributor like Gardners can help you to gain supplier agreements with larger retailers. They do have particular terms so do your research first.

www.nielsentitleeditor.com/titleeditor/

www.gardners.com

Tip #8: Pre-launch strategy

Tell everyone that you are writing a book (keep the exact content a secret), you never know the invitations that may arise!

You may choose to make your book available on Amazon for a period of time before you officially launch your book. During this period ask your friends and connections to read your book and get ready to do reviews on launch day. Start your marketing campaign in the pre-launch period with exciting 'coming soon' messaging.

Tip #9: Mailing list

Do you have a Facebook page, Facebook group, Instagram profile or mailing list? Think about how you can reach your audience and keep a dialogue going with them. Offer tips and post an advert for your book every six posts, the other five giving value or creating discussion.

- Offer review copies.
- Give away free copies for awareness days.
- Create business birthday giveaways and offers.

Remember, with your mailing list it's all about giving value and being consistent. Plan a calendar of 6-12 months' worth of content ideas so you aren't scratching around for ideas with a deadline!

Tip #10: Mini intro video of you/your book

People buy people! Create a video with you and your book, explaining why you wrote it and what it is about.

Remember, videos also attract attention on social media. Take your time to create the right environment, wear your favourite clothes and enjoy the experience of telling people about your book.

Hate being on camera? Create a video or reel showing your book in fun locations, or get a few of your readers to do a video review. Or take a deep breath and do it anyway – this is your book and you deserve to be seen with it! Be excited about your book to get everyone else excited! Film it, photograph it – choose fun backgrounds, add music and maybe captions too.

PROMOTION STRATEGY ONE: REBECCA JENKINS

So, you've completed the herculean task of writing of your book.

Big congratulations.

Now the hard work starts!

I know, just when you thought you could take a break!

Regrettably not yet! Now you must switch roles from author to chief marketer and attract readers. Let me rephrase that more accurately, you have to market, market, market your book at every opportunity and you need a strategy to do it.

I'd like to share with you how my book has become the recommended read for sales teams and account managers at a global business. How it generates clients for my company, even without them reading my book.

This is how I use my book as an effective marketing tool.

At first, I thought an experienced publicist would be all that I needed to promote my book. Whilst I gained a good number of PR opportunities, radio interviews and featured in publications, I realised that it wouldn't be a sustainable strategy for the long term.

That's when I began to appreciate that I needed to shift my thinking and use my book as part of my overall business marketing strategy. Rather than focusing on promoting my book as a standalone.

This shift in thinking helped me to see the value of my book differently. As a result, I decided to give my book away for free to potential clients.

Yes, I know what you might be thinking, all that hard work and you give your book away!

Let me explain…

By giving my book to the right people, in my case business executives and decision makers, it has opened doors, and it's been a key component in an integrated marketing strategy.

My book has become a point of influence in a prospect's journey to become a client of my business. It is an effective way to increase engagement and build a relationship with them.

If I just promoted the book on Amazon, without this approach, I would have no knowledge of who purchased it, and therefore unable to engage with them.

When I give my book away for free, even if a recipient only reads the back cover, they learn about my business experience which immediately positions my expertise. You can see how this becomes a powerful point of influence in the buyer's experience with my business.

In addition to this, I use social media. I create articles about the key topics in my book and explain that followers can gain further insights by reading my book, and they can

50 Ways To Promote Your Book

get a free copy at my website.

This has many advantages, they may look around my website to find out more, for example read client success stories, and see what we offer.

To send them a free copy of my book, I need their contact details. Once they have provided their information the book is sent, along with an automated sequence of informative emails that support the book's principles. I also offer a strategy call to see how they can effectively use the methods in my book to improve their ability to find, gain and grow clients for their business.

You can see how I position my book on the home page of my website (www.RJEN.co.uk).

In summary, my recommendation is to think of your book as part of a bigger and integrated marketing strategy. One that generates a greater return by giving it away for free, over hoping it gets found on Amazon!

50 Ways To Promote Your Book

I wish you every success in marketing your book.

GET EXCITED!

Tip #11: Launch your book!

Pick a date and launch your book. This can be in person or online, or preferably both! Remember to invite as many people as possible, ask for reviews and get photos. You can use all of this collateral to promote your book later.

Your launch date could be a special date to you, or you could raise your social media presence by piggybacking off of a relevant awareness day, like International Women's Day, Stress Awareness Month...anything that will attract the attention of your audience.

Whenever you pick, allow plenty of time to promote it, invite as many people as you can (as some won't attend on the day) and most important of all – enjoy it, you've worked hard to get this book to print!

Tip #12: Un-boxing video

A fun way to show people your new book is to do an un-boxing video. Tell your audience about your book and that this is the first time you will be seeing it. Film yourself opening the box and seeing your book for the first time, or get someone to film it for you. Remember to wave the book around, show inside and give your audience a close up of it.

Show people your happy and excited face!

This can be a great way of building some buzz around your book ahead of your launch, people love a feel good story.

Tip #13: Take pictures!

Get pictures of people reading your book/taking your book to interesting places. You can use these on social media, with or without quotes from the people, as pictures attract attention. This will show social proof that people are enjoying your book and also create the visual to your potential reader that they too can enjoy your book on holiday, on the train…or in the bath!

Tip #14: Book signings and book readings

Celebrate your book!

Arrange your own event: share your keynote and invite other experts in your niche to speak. Ask them to share details of the event and your book to their audience.

If you are holding an event that you are running on your own, choose a venue that suits your book and remember to use a special pen for book signing!

Independent bookshops may be open to hosting your event which will widen your book's reach, be brave and reach out to your local ones, the worst that can happen is that they say no and if you don't ask, it's a no anyway!

However you do it, remember to have a stock of books to sell, take photos and use them on your social media. Remember to enjoy it too!

Tip #15: Book reviews: part 1

Forward copies of your book to people who might be interested in writing a review on Amazon and also sharing their thoughts on social media or with their wider group. This could be another expert in your niche, or someone with a similar demographic that you admire. Remember to put a copy of their review on your book website or Facebook page and share them on your socials as you receive them.

Every interaction keeps the momentum up and creates more of a buzz about your book. Don't be shy, shout your successes from the rooftops!

Tip #16: Book reviews: part 2

If someone tells you they have bought your book on Amazon, reach out and ask them to leave a review. This helps the algorithm on your book and you can share this on social media. Aim to get at least 15 reviews of your book. You can also email your newsletter list and offer free PDF copies in return for a review.

Tip #17: Book reviews: part 3

Submit your book to Booksprout and NetGalley for independent reviews of your book. Also, the Goodreads author program allows you to create a profile page to share details of you and your books, ask for reviews, host discussions and add your books to relevant lists.

How often have you checked out the reviews of a hotel on TripAdvisor before booking? Book reviews are the same. They are social proof that your book is great. They also give you marketing collateral for your social media, both for this book and any subsequent book.

Tip #18: Quotes from the book

Take quotes from the book and put them on visuals for social media. You could put them alongside a picture of you and/or your book. Remember to include the name of your book and the picture on the visual, if there is room. You can use Canva or other apps to make your visuals stand out and remember to keep within your brand colours. If this isn't your thing, get a graphic designer to help you.

There is a 'rule of seven' in marketing. It is said that your customer needs to see your product seven times before they buy. Great eye-catching visuals spark curiosity in your book.

THE BOUNCE BACK
JOURNEY OF
WOMEN'S HEALTH

AN INSPIRING COLLECTION
OF PERSONAL STORIES

Available on Amazon!

☆☆☆☆☆
Reviewed in the United Kingdom on 16 October 2020
A must read for anyone who faces a challenge and needs inspiration on overcoming it.
Within this book is a collection of personal stories of women from all walks of life who have overcome a challenge in one form or another. I have found every single story in this book to be inspirational. Thank you ladies for sharing your stories with the world.

#socialpassionproject

Discover Your Bounce
Publishing

Tip #19: Reels

Reels are a great way of reaching your audience. You can share them on TikTok, Facebook and Instagram, saving you time by repurposing the same content over and over.

You can share snippets from your book launch, updates when your book gets to best seller, reviews and any other content that connects you to your audience.

Try a mix of short form and longer videos, record in various locations and have fun experimenting to find what works for you. Remember to add descriptions and hashtags, and tag in people that may share.

Tip #20: Celebrity collaborations

Ask someone who is well known in your sector for a quote about your book – it adds extra credence to what you have produced. If they agree, ask them to share it with their community or following too.

In our book, The Bounce Back Journey of Men's Health, TV personality Martyn Roberts kindly wrote the foreword. He is passionate about promoting good mental health and we were so thrilled when he joined us for the online launch. We repeated this for The Bounce Back Journey of Parenting when Grammy award winning song writer Marvee Woods wrote the foreword and shared his story of becoming a parent.

50 Ways To Promote Your Book

PROMOTION STRATEGY TWO: JENNY LEWIS

'TikTok made me buy it.'

Ha!

If there's one thing that'll immediately put me off buying a book, it's 'TikTok made me buy it' somewhere in the promotional blurb.

Proof, if you needed it, that not all marketing works on all readers, and not all marketing works for all writers.

The joy of marketing (it is there, honest) is in experimentation. Reading books like this, learning the so-called rules, and then using that as a foundation to figure out what's right for you.

I don't like being in the limelight, receiving reviews terrifies me and the idea of building a social media presence makes me feel physically sick.

My experience of attempting to build that social media

presence hasn't been all bad. But every sale has come with having to cultivate a specific and lengthy relationship with every individual who bought my books. While I've made a few amazing friends, this just isn't practical if your aim is to sell thousands.

Being an anti-social shadow-dweller, I hate to admit that building your own mailing list can work wonders. It has some major drawbacks (what do you write in those emails, how often, everyone just wants freebies!) but my mailing list has resulted in a five-star review declaring that my paranormal fantasy series should be made into a Netflix series (still my favourite review ever), and a conversation with another mailing list reader who demanded that my seven-book sci-fi/fantasy series be longer after only reading the first book.

The paid newsletter method – paying a company with genre specific lists of thousands of readers to promote your discounted book – can work wonders if done correctly. Although you need to figure out which lists are experiencing good engagement for your genre at that moment, which can prove quite costly, especially as to be done well, they need to be staggered (unless you can land the elusive BookBub promotion).

The best thing I ever did for my book marketing, however, were Amazon ads. That dashboard is terrifying, especially when you're clueless. I avoided it for a long time. It wasn't until I had a back catalogue of ten books and was twiddling my thumbs during a pandemic that I took the plunge to learn the system.

There are a lot of books and courses on the subject, but I went with Bryan Cohen's free challenge, which he runs throughout the year. For one week, I absorbed and applied everything.

My sales, downloads and income immediately shot up. Writers think Amazon ads will cost them too much, but I only started to make a (tiny) loss when I took a break from publishing and marketing, and the momentum began to die.

There are other marketing methods that I'm eager to try, so my best advice to any author is to learn what's out there and then experiment. See what works for you and what doesn't. See what suits you and makes you feel good, and what doesn't. Don't go against your gut, because you don't need to. There are plenty of ways of making this dream work and it looks different for everyone, so go out and find your way.

Find Jenny's fantasy books at www.amazon.co.uk/J-E-Nice/e/B01M13O6P7 and her romance books at www.amazon.co.uk/Jennifer-Nice/e/B08P3TRM66

KEEP GOING!

Tip #21: Bulk purchases

Which organisations would love to have bulk copies of your book at a small discount? Consider:

- Universities

- Event organisers

- People that run groups in your niche

- Book clubs

- Charities

Choose to offer a bulk buy discount that is between the author copy price and Recommended Retail Price. Offering this could also lead to keynote or workshop opportunities. Create a list of people you can contact and reach out to them. You may want to include a photo and bio to make it more personal.

Tip #22: Tips to camera from your book

Share relevant snippets from your book to give your audience a taste of what to expect when they read your book. Make them 15 seconds or less and post on your socials, add into your emails and create reels. To save time you may want to create several videos at the same time and drip feed them.

You can also make videos of the reviews you have received; some people prefer watching video!

Tip #23: Podcasts

If your book supports your business, why not have a podcast series! Interview people about topics in the book that you have covered. You can take snippets from the podcast for use on YouTube and your socials if you record the audio using Zoom or similar.

Having a podcast demonstrates your expertise and gives you another reason to talk about your book. A podcast also gives you access to a new audience as many people love listening on their commute or at the gym.

Offer to speak on other people's podcasts and use their audiences to spread the word too. Take a look at www.podcastguests.com for podcast opportunities. Also check out Facebook groups for opportunities to take part on podcasts or on Facebook lives.

Tip #24: Keynote opportunities

Design a 10 minute, 20 minute and a 45 minute talk to share around the subject of your book. This is a great way to highlight your knowledge and position yourself as an authority in your area of expertise. Many authors find their revenue comes from keynotes and workshops as well as book sales.

- 10 or 20 minute talk - present it for free in networking and community groups
- 45 minute talk - know your value and charge a fee!

Remember to share details of how to buy your book at every one, it doesn't have to be a lengthy pitch, just a mention.

If the event is ticketed, include the cost of a book in the price. Or have a stand at the event and sell your books separately, perhaps with a discount or two for one offer as an incentive to immediately buy.

Tip #25: Share snippets from your book launch

Having an online book launch? Remember to record it! Zoom and Teams both have recording options.

Use snippets of the video with people sharing what they love about your book. These can be used on YouTube, Instagram, Twitter, Facebook, TikTok etc. Use some as short form video, and bring several together to create longer content.

Video is preferred by most algorithms and it's social proof that your book is fabulous (which of course it is!).

Tip #26: Networking

Most networking groups have a 10 minute slot where you can talk about your book or your business to give value to the attendees. Initially, visit networking groups as a guest and choose a mix of online and in-person events to see which you prefer or feel comfortable in. Even if your book is a novel, they may still be interested to hear how you wrote it!

Remember, there are general networks for business owners, as well as niche networks like The Law Society, property networks, networks for the construction industry and men or women only groups. There are so many networks to choose from, find a few that work for you and concentrate on turning up regularly and giving value.

Tip #27: Debates between characters

You can introduce your characters online and tell your readers about them. Your characters could be linked to something topical, like the winner of a TV competition. Ask your readers who they think your character would prefer to win and why. This works well for fiction books but can also be used for business books where opposing views or approaches are compared.

If you have a Facebook group for your book or business, use this platform for debates between fictional characters too. What would your characters say? Does your audience have a favourite? Bestselling authors Stacey Campbell and Tracy Firks did this really well with their book The Director. They created Team Liam and Team Cameron so people could choose their favourite of the two leading male characters. They had great fun on socials and you can too – this book promoting doesn't always need to be serious!

Tip #28: Special days

Have a strategy around using media of all types on days which are relevant to your book. Remember, journalists are always looking for stories, for example if yours is a business book, think of an angle around the tax deadline or the budget.

You can have great fun on social media too.

For a romance novel, Valentine's Day is a must, if your fiction hero has autism then use Autism Awareness Day. Add your slant and be creative on these days – where could your book be used? Your book with a red rose for Valentine's or with a calculator for tax return deadline day. Photograph your book in the hands of lovely ladies who are pleased to be unwrapping your book on Mother's day, or pose your book with an Easter Egg.

Christmas is a great opportunity to have some fun. It

could be read by an elf, or Santa Claus himself! It could be under a Christmas tree or stage a pile of your books in Santa's sleigh.

Tip #29: Influencer endorsements

Send a copy of your book to an influencer in your field. Ask for a review and preferably a picture of them with your book.

Sometimes Imposter Syndrome can sneak in here, but take a big breath and contact the person/people you really admire. Perhaps connect with them on social media first and comment on their posts so they know who you are. Or choose someone in your network who is already known to them to introduce you.

Remember, nothing ventured, nothing gained!

Tip #30: Paid for adverts

Amazon ads are a great way of getting your book in front of a wider audience, Amazon will suggest your book to people searching for your chosen keywords or categories.

There is an investment in doing this and perhaps you will get an expert to do this for you. Promoting your book yourself with social media and networking may be the only strategy you use, but ads can work really well if you have the time, the expertise and the budget.

PROMOTION STRATEGY THREE: HELEN BLENKINSOPP

After writing and publishing nine thriller novels since 2013, I now understand the secret of success. You only need two things: a great book and a way to tell readers about it.

While that sounds simple, how do you know a book will sell and how do you get it in front of readers? There are four key ingredients in the recipe:

1. Writing the best story you can and having it professionally edited.

2. An obvious genre.

3. A cover appropriate for that genre.

4. Amazon advertising.

You can also improve your chances with a well-written book description and a professional-looking format.

If only I'd known in 2013. Let's draw a veil over my

first, unedited book (I subsequently paid for an edit, then bought and pulped any used copies I could find). Let's forget, too, about the covers designed by a cleaner, a cloakroom attendant and a graduate fresh out of art school. These artists had talent, but they didn't understand commercial book design. When I realised this and bought new covers, sales improved. Get it right first time: go to professionals like Elizabeth Mackey or Miblart.

Once you have a well-presented book, it's time to reach out to strangers. Some authors use Facebook ads for this. Personally, I regard Facebook as a black hole into which I pour money. It's easy to make a mistake when setting up an ad, break for lunch and discover two hours later that Facebook has helped itself to £20 from your bank account. Nor is it certain that a reader browsing cat pictures would be tempted to buy a book. Amazon, on the other hand, is where readers go to buy.

The gamechanger for me was Bryan Cohen's free training on Amazon advertising. I learned that Amazon ads are charged on a cost per click basis. You set a maximum amount you're prepared to pay for a click. This is your bid. Amazon effectively runs an auction for the ad space. When your bid wins, Amazon shows your book to readers. They may have searched for, say, "psychological thrillers with unpredictable twists." Amazon will show them a page of books, including yours. Readers will only twig they are seeing an ad if they spot the word "Sponsored" in tiny letters. At this stage, Amazon is giving you free advertising. You pay nothing until somebody clicks on your book.

Bryan believes in testing the market with low bids. Higher bidders are likely to see their books advertised more often. They are also likely to run out of money, as not every click results in a sale. Low bids are a long game, but they preserve your cash and give you the best chance of making profits.

I first tried Amazon ads on my Trail series, a mash-up of psychological thriller, crime and mystery stories. Sales were boosted, but the ads really came into their own when I launched a straight-down-the-line psychological thriller Bright Lies. This tale of a wicked stepfather gathered 150 preorders and charted in Amazon's hot new releases. It's much easier to advertise a book when the genre is obvious.

At the time of writing, Bryan runs his free courses for two weeks every quarter. He has also written several self-help books for authors. Do check them out by using the "Look Inside" feature on Amazon. While you're there, if you love a psychological thriller with unpredictable twists, look no further than my latest, Lies at Her Door.

She longed for excitement. Big mistake. Now she's accused of murder and fighting for her life…

Find Helen's books at www.amazon.co.uk/AA-Abbott/e/B00DXKBFUI

TIME FOR A REFRESH?

Tip #31: Refresh your book

Time moves on and so do your reader's expectations.

Does your book need a refresh? Is the cover in need of some TLC? Consider a new cover and relaunch your book. Consider asking for more endorsements or including the reviews you received the first time you launched on the back cover.

Is there anything you could update?

If you wrote your book a while ago and there are more chapters or revised chapters, you can create a second edition of the book.

A new version can be a great way to engage with people. Ask your potential readers to choose your book cover from three options you have had created. This creates engagement and they may see something that you haven't. After all, they are the ones who you want to be compelled to buy your book and this will help them to feel invested in it.

Tip #32: Relaunch your book!

If your book is already in circulation there is no reason why you can't launch it again. This could be in person or online and could coincide with a new service you are offering, a business birthday or a reduced price offer.

Even if your book has been out a while, your audience will have changed and grown. Amazon will have 'lost interest' in your book in favour of new books published, but with a little effort and a strategy you can change this. Nicky's book, Rescued By The Coastguard, re-charted two years after its initial launch and featured next to Michelle Obama's book.

Tip #33: Put your book on offer for a weekend/week to celebrate

Is there an anniversary you could celebrate which is relevant to your book? For example, are there any awareness days that are applicable, is it your birthday or the anniversary of the launch of your book or business?

Get ready in advance, prepare all of your social posts and let your list know you are doing an offer. Ideally spend 3–6 weeks planning in advance. This will give your publisher time to update the price and set the timescales on your book platform, and you can plan out your posts without a rush. Once the price is updated share your posts with your link. Share any new reviews and pictures of new readers with your book.

Tip #34: Facebook groups

Facebook groups are a great way to connect with a wider audience of people in your niche. Choose relevant groups and raise your profile by commenting and giving value. When the group invites you to share offers, add in your book link. Remember to not just 'drop and run', choose the number of groups that you have time to interact with and spend time getting to know people.

Some groups interview their members, so keep a look out for chances to appear on lives and talk about your book/niche. Share your reviews and remind anyone who has read your book to leave a review.

Create bundle offers of your book with courses/coaching or whatever you sell and post these when you are invited – don't spam, it won't help your reputation.

You can put adverts for your book in groups, but try not to overdo it, people don't like being sold to! However, if you have an offer – a reduction in price for a few days, for example – let people know.

As well as being a member of other groups, build your own!

A Facebook group is a great place to invite your readers and online connections. This is a great way to position yourself as a thought leader, showcase your chosen topic and create discussion and debates around the topics of your book/niche.

Tip #35: Local radio

Approach your local radio station with a story about your book. Presenters and researchers love stories about local people doing amazing things. Check out the show most likely to fit with your reader/audience and approach the presenter.

Remember to share your appearance on your social media before the event and the replay afterwards. There are a huge array of internet radio stations too, so look for niche radio stations to approach.

It can be helpful to have a press release with the relevant information, along with your image and biography — make it easy for people to engage with you.

Tip #36: Local newspaper

Approach your local newspaper with a story about your book. Did a local landmark inspire the book? What local context can you give? Bookstores and libraries in your region may also be interested if there is a local reference or link.

Prepare a press release or get a PR company to work with you. Keep it interesting and short, put the most important information or hook in the first couple of lines, remember journalists are short of time. Add your contact details and be ready to respond quickly, there could be a deadline.

If your story is printed, remember to share on your social media and newsletter.

Tip #37: Charity fundraising

Is there a charity that aligns with your book? Could you offer to do a talk, maybe sell some books and give some of the profits to that charity? Research local and national charities and reach out to a few for an initial conversation about what would work best.

Supporting a charity creates multiple wins: the charity benefits, you align your profile to a great cause and you create more collateral to use in promoting your book.

Remember to document the event on social media, take photos and tag in the charity to raise awareness of the good work they do!

Tip #38: Trade fairs and conferences

Where is your audience going to be this year? Be there too!

If you have written a business book, you could approach relevant conferences as a speaker, or to have a stand. Some conferences are general local business events, some are specialist events such as accounting or law, so pick those relevant to your audience. Business fairs and expos can provide opportunities for speaking; some may ask for a fee, so weigh up the opportunity and investment.

If the purpose of your book is to bring people to your business, consider providing a free copy to all delegates. You can also create competitions for people who buy your book – ask them to email their receipt to be entered – this is a great way to list build (remember to comply with GDPR).

Tip #39: Endorsement by volume

As we have mentioned before, encourage your readers to post pictures of themselves with your book, but also create a unique hashtag for them to use. To create a buzz around your book you can find and reshare the pictures with the hashtag and thank your readers for choosing your book. Ask them what they liked about it, create threads and discussions for other potential readers to see.

Why not set up an extreme reading challenge? Encourage people to post photos of themselves reading your book in unusual places such as up a mountain or in a swimming pool.

Both of these ideas are fun to do, they create eye-catching content and interrupts the scrolling! They also build community.

50 Ways To Promote Your Book

Tip #40: Independent bookstores

If you don't get time when you launch, later on you can still approach independent bookstores with your book and ask if they would like you to do a book reading, book signing etc. Some book shops will refuse books published on Amazon, but some will welcome your book. Make a list of the book shops you would love to stock your book and then pay them a visit or give them a call.

Don't be put off if some say no, keep going and visualise your book sitting on the shelf before you visit. You may offer a discount for a bulk order of your books and some smaller shops will ask about sale or return. If you have a series of events planned this may work for you, but only say yes to the terms you are happy with.

PROMOTON STRATEGY FOUR: RICH COLLIS

When I had the fantastic news that my book would be published, I knew that I would need to start an 'online presence'. I set up public Instagram and Facebook pages dedicated to my writing and book, which would help bring people on my journey to publishing with me and gather interest through a more personal insight. With my social media posts I made sure I utilised popular book hashtags (#booktok, #bookstagram, #bookstagramuk, #books) so that my posts could reach a wider audience. I also ensured that I responded to all comments left on my pages so that these appeared on people's feeds. This was my main source of marketing during the writing and editing phase, and I tried to post every week.

As my book has a target audience of older teens I knew that TikTok would be a medium that I would need to at least attempt to embrace as this would be an area that my target market would be using, and I needed to be visible here. I posted my first TikTok video on the day that my book was put into print (using the same hashtags as my Facebook and Instagram posts) and have since tried to post a new video on TikTok every few weeks. I have found that, whilst I get plenty of views of my videos, there is very little interaction here. You can pay to 'promote' on the site (where your video becomes played to more people) but I do not know if this has any impact on sales. I am, however, very aware that I am a novice in this area so there is much I could probably still do to promote myself on the app!

Once my book had been released on Amazon, I decided that the best way to get past the 'friends and family' boundary of sales was to go the old-fashioned way and visit bookshops with a copy of the book and a letter. In each store I went to in my local city centre I asked to speak to the duty manager and spoke to them about being a local author, asking whether they would support me by stocking the book for sale. The responses and results were mixed; some were very congratulatory and said they would 'see what they could do' and some were outright dismissive. I learnt that Waterstones have an area on their website for independently published authors where you can alert them to your new book and this brings it to the attention of head office and the various regional buyers (top tip!) – this, along with a visit to my nearest stores, is my latest hope for increasing sales.

Personally, I have found the marketing harder than the writing. You need to dedicate time to it and have a thick skin. But do not see it as a chore – many people would love to be in the position of having a book published, so embrace the challenge!

Find Rich's books at www.amazon.co.uk/Richard-Collis/e/B0BLHXXRV1

MORE AMAZING IDEAS

Tip #41: Articles

Written a book? Then why not write some more!

Create articles about your topic and approach the media with relevant articles on an aspect of the book. For a novel, write about the context or your research for the book, for example advice for singles going back into dating if you have written a novel around that topic.

Choose a mix of mainstream media and magazines or smaller publications around your niche. Local media can be a great place to start.

Remember to include your book link and website or socials at the end of each article. If you have an Amazon Author Central profile this is a great link to share.

Articles work really well on LinkedIn too, so while you are waiting for a media response share different articles on your own profile.

Tip #42: Book giveaway

This works well for inspirational books, but can work for all sorts of books, people love a random gift! Wrap some of your books and leave them in public places for people to pick up. Leave a note saying, "If you have found this book, it belongs to you. Take it home and enjoy it. If you feel that you can support me, please leave a review at…or share a photo of you with the book on social media with…hashtag."

You can also use the giveaway on socials to ask where would be a good place to leave your book. Follow up with a picture of where you have left it.

Love bombing – get your friends to help! Who needs your book? Maybe ask on social media and if you get a lot of responses, do a draw online for your book or books.

Competitions – give away a selection of your books

and get people to enter a competition, perhaps a caption competition from a photo or to answer a question around your subject. Remember to follow guidelines on social media and be clear on the rules of entry.

Tip #43: Book discounting sites

BookBub and BookGorilla are examples of book discounting and recommendation services.

BookBub is for ebooks. Their subscribers receive regular emails recommending titles. You will have to offer your book for free or for a large discount for a limited period but it can help with reviews and getting your book seen.

You submit your title by completing the online form, then BookBub does a review. If you are selected, you will receive confirmation and an invoice. You will have to co-ordinate the price reduction across your retailers, but BookBub prepare your promotion and send it to their readers. The price reduction will typically need to be a 70% reduction or more.

BookGorilla offer a free author page with a short bio

and you add in your books which are on promotion.

BookGorilla send out daily alerts of relevant books to your target market.

Links to explore:

www.bookbub.com

www.partners.bookbub.com/users/sign_in

www.bookgorilla.com

Tip #44: Other events

Look out for opportunities to speak at events. Also contact people with the same target audience and enquire after speaking opportunities. Book festivals and independent book shops may be useful for this, as well as opportunities posted on social media.

Being invited to join a panel to debate a topic is useful for raising your profile and getting a business book in front of a new audience. Look out for business shows or online events that may be looking for panel members.

Why not create your own panel too? Ask people who have the same audience but a different niche or message to join you to discuss your topic.

Tip #45: Awards

Awards are a great way to raise your profile and get recognition for what you do. You can enter yourself for most awards or ask a friend or PR expert to do it.

Take time to ensure you have answered all the entry questions fully, be proud of your achievements; don't hold back.

Choose a range of awards: book awards, industry awards as well as local and national awards. Share when you are shortlisted and when you attend events too, this will boost your visibility and lead to other opportunities.

Tip #46: Public relations

Journalists are always looking for good content, so create a press release about your book or why your content is needed in your niche. Take time thinking about the value you can give, a relevant angle and why a journalist would share your book. Contact relevant national newspapers and magazines as well as niche publications and your local press.

Remember to make it easy for the journalist to print your words; correct any typos and share your website, socials and contact information.

There are groups on Facebook where media people ask for stories, like Feature Me and Pitch and Shout. Also follow #journorequest on Twitter. If you are unsure of what to write, contact PR companies to enlist professional help.

Tip #47: TEDx

The TED or TEDx stage is a great place to raise your profile. Use an element of your personal story to create an 18 minute presentation idea, this will need to be a concept worth sharing or a new idea, so take your time watching some past TED talks on YouTube. Once accepted, TEDx offer great speaker training, so you will be supported right up to the event.

Look online for a list of events and choose a few that would work for you.

Tip #48: Keep promoting your book!

…Even a year after launch you can still promote your book!

Promoting your book is not a one off activity. Create a marketing strategy for your book. Consider what activities you are engaged in every month that support ongoing promotion. Some promotional strategies are seasonal, some are linked to activities such as book signings and some can be regular strategies. Try to run a campaign every 90 days.

It can be hard thinking of new ideas, so maybe look at what other authors are doing for inspiration and then create your own unique content.

Tip #49: Try a new social media platform

Always on Facebook? Try Instagram or TikTok…

It's good to get known on one or two channels and to focus your attention there, but if you feel you want to grow your audience, get to know another channel. Perhaps you are daunted by TikTok, or flummoxed by Instagram? There are many experts and tutorials to help you, so put aside some time and learn something new.

Choose a channel that works for your content, for example Pinterest if you have something physical like a book!

As we have already mentioned, if you are going to do it, be consistent for at least three months to see if it works for you.

Tip #50: Love your book!

Keep the faith that your book is amazing, that the time you invested will be of value to others and hold it in your heart with great affection.

There are phases we go through as authors. Remember the excitement of starting to write and the pride when you have written something well? The editing process can be tough and can take up your energy but promoting your book takes time and patience and needs to happen even if you are fed up with the sight of your book!

So, think back to the start of your journey and remember the highlights. Remember your first great review, the joy of holding (and sniffing!) your finished book and the lovely comments from friends and family. Fall back in love with your book.

BONUS STRATEGY: JOEL STONE
How to Promote Yourself as an Author

So, you've written a book. Congratulations! You've poured your heart, soul and probably a lot of coffee into those pages. But now what? How do you get people to read it? The answer is simple – promote yourself as an author. And no, that doesn't mean awkwardly slipping your book into every conversation.

As a marketing entrepreneur, international speaker and best selling co-author of Stay Hungry, I know a thing or two about promoting yourself as an author. So, buckle up, my fellow writers, because I'm about to drop some knowledge bombs on you.

Gather reviews

Let's start with the basics. Reviews are the lifeblood of any book. They help to build credibility, increase visibility and convince potential readers that your book is worth their time and money.

Now, I know what you're thinking – "But Joel, how do I get reviews if nobody has read my book yet?" Fear not, my friend, I have a solution.

Reach out to your family, friends, colleagues and even your high school English teacher. Offer them a free copy of your book in exchange for an honest review. You can also join book clubs or author groups on social media and offer to exchange reviews with other authors.

And don't forget about book bloggers and bookstagrammers. These influencers love to read and review books, and they have a built-in audience of readers who trust their opinions. Reach out to them and ask if they'd be interested in reviewing your book.

Guest on podcasts

Podcasts are a fantastic way to promote yourself and your book. Not only do they have a loyal following of listeners, but they also give you the opportunity to showcase your personality, expertise and writing style.

But here's the thing – you can't just sit around waiting for podcast hosts to invite you on their show. You have to be proactive and pitch yourself.

Do some research and find podcasts that align with your genre or niche. Listen to a few episodes and get a feel for the host's style and audience. Then, reach out to the host and pitch yourself as a guest. Highlight why you'd be a great fit for their show, and don't forget to mention your book.

Speaking from the stage

Speaking from the stage is another powerful way to promote yourself and your book. It gives you the opportunity to connect with your audience, share your story and showcase your expertise.

Now, I know speaking in public can be terrifying for some people. But here's a secret – even the most confident speakers get nervous. The key is to practise, practise, practise.

Start small by speaking at local libraries or bookstores. Join a public speaking club like Toastmasters to hone your skills. And don't forget to bring copies of your book to sell after your talk.

Not being shy to tell people you've written a book

Last but not least, don't be shy to tell people you've written a book. I know it can be uncomfortable to talk about yourself and your accomplishments, but you have to get over it.

Imagine you're at a networking event, and someone

asks you what you do. Instead of saying, "Oh, I'm just a writer," say, "I'm an author, and I've just published my first book." See the difference?

You don't have to be pushy or salesy. Just be proud of your book and confident in yourself. And who knows, maybe that person you're talking to is a book lover and will be eager to check out your work.

Good luck promoting your book!

Find Joel's books at www.amazon.co.uk/Joel-Stone/e/B092SQ3DZF

ABOUT DISCOVER YOUR BOUNCE!

Discover Your Bounce is a group of companies to provide a platform for wellbeing and inspiration, to support each other and to learn from our collective experience.

Discover Your Bounce Publishing specialises in inspirational stories and business books. We provide writing courses, mentoring for authors and support from inception of your idea through writing, publishing and managing your book launch. If you have an idea for a book, or a part written manuscript that you want to get over the line, contact Nicky or Sharon on the links below.

Discover Your Bounce For Business provides support for employers who want to improve the staff wellbeing, engagement, culture and performance of their business.

We work with CEOs, HR Managers or department heads to deliver workshops with practical, easy to implement techniques that create instant change. As we go to print, we are working with employees across the globe from a variety of industries and have delivered keynotes at some fantastic international conferences and events.

My Wellbeing supports individuals through mentoring and online courses to improve their energy and vision. If your get up and go has got up and gone, get in touch and get bouncing!

Sharon and Nicky are available to discuss speaking opportunities, wellbeing workshops or private mentoring:

Nicky@discoveryourbounce.com
Sharon@discoveryourbounce.com

You can also find out more on our website:
https://www.discoveryourbounce.com

Join Our Communities!

For wellbeing inspiration and positivity:

www.facebook.com/groups/discoveryourbouncecommunity

For book lovers:

www.facebook.com/groups/bouncybooks

The Bounce Back Journey Series

The original Bounce Back Journey was published in February 2020, when we had no idea of the challenges that were to come. The series includes The Bounce Back Journey of Women's Health, The Bounce Back Journey of

Men's Health, The Bounce Back Journey of Careers and The Bounce Back Journey of Parenting. All books are available on Kindle and in Paperback on Amazon.

Social Passion Project

Royalties from these books fund our Social Passion Project, providing mental health awareness training and supporting other important mental health projects. Read more at:

www.discoveryourbounce.com/social-passion-project.

ABOUT THE AUTHORS

Nicky Marshall

Nicky is an award winning, international speaker and best-selling author. She is also a mum, nan and wife and loves nothing more than family time.

At 40, Nicky suffered and recovered from a disabling stroke – inspiring a life's mission to make a bigger difference.

Nicky has an accountancy background and twenty years of helping people improve their health and wellbeing under her belt. Combining both, Nicky is a mentor, seasoned workplace facilitator and keynote speaker,

50 Ways To Promote Your Book

inspiring people to discover their own brand of Bounce! Nicky's knowledge, knack for stress busting, hugs and infectious laugh make her an in demand and popular speaker.

With passion in buckets and a penchant for keeping it simple, Nicky has a unique talent in breaking down the barriers that hold people back from living a life they love.

Be careful if you stand too close - her enthusiasm rubs off!

Follow these links to connect with Nicky:

www.discoveryourbounce.com

www.facebook.com/discoveryourbounce

www.twitter.com/_nickymarshall

www.instagram.com/nickymarshalldyb

www.sleek.bio/nickymarshall

Or send her an e-mail:

Nicky@discoveryourbounce.com

Sharon Critchlow

Sharon is one to watch! As an international best-selling writer and speaker Sharon is a vocal changemaker. She brings passion to the subjects of the future of work, diversity, emotional intelligence and environmental social governance.

Sharon is a qualified Accountant with over 20 years of experience in senior leadership roles and growing successful businesses. Within Discover Your Bounce, Sharon looks after the finances and provides strategic direction for the group. She is a popular conference speaker as well as regularly creating and facilitating workshops. A qualified coach and mentor, Sharon is passionate about people becoming the best that they can be and allowing their true talents to shine.

In her spare time Sharon is an Advocate for the Association of Chartered Certified Accountants (ACCA) encouraging people into the profession and supporting their development. She also enjoys music and has been known to play the flute and sing – although not at the same time!

Website: www.discoveryourbounce.com

Email : Sharon@discoveryourbounce.com

LinkedIn: www.linkedin.com/in/sharoncritchlow

Twitter: @sharoncritchlow

Printed in Great Britain
by Amazon

59186775R00067